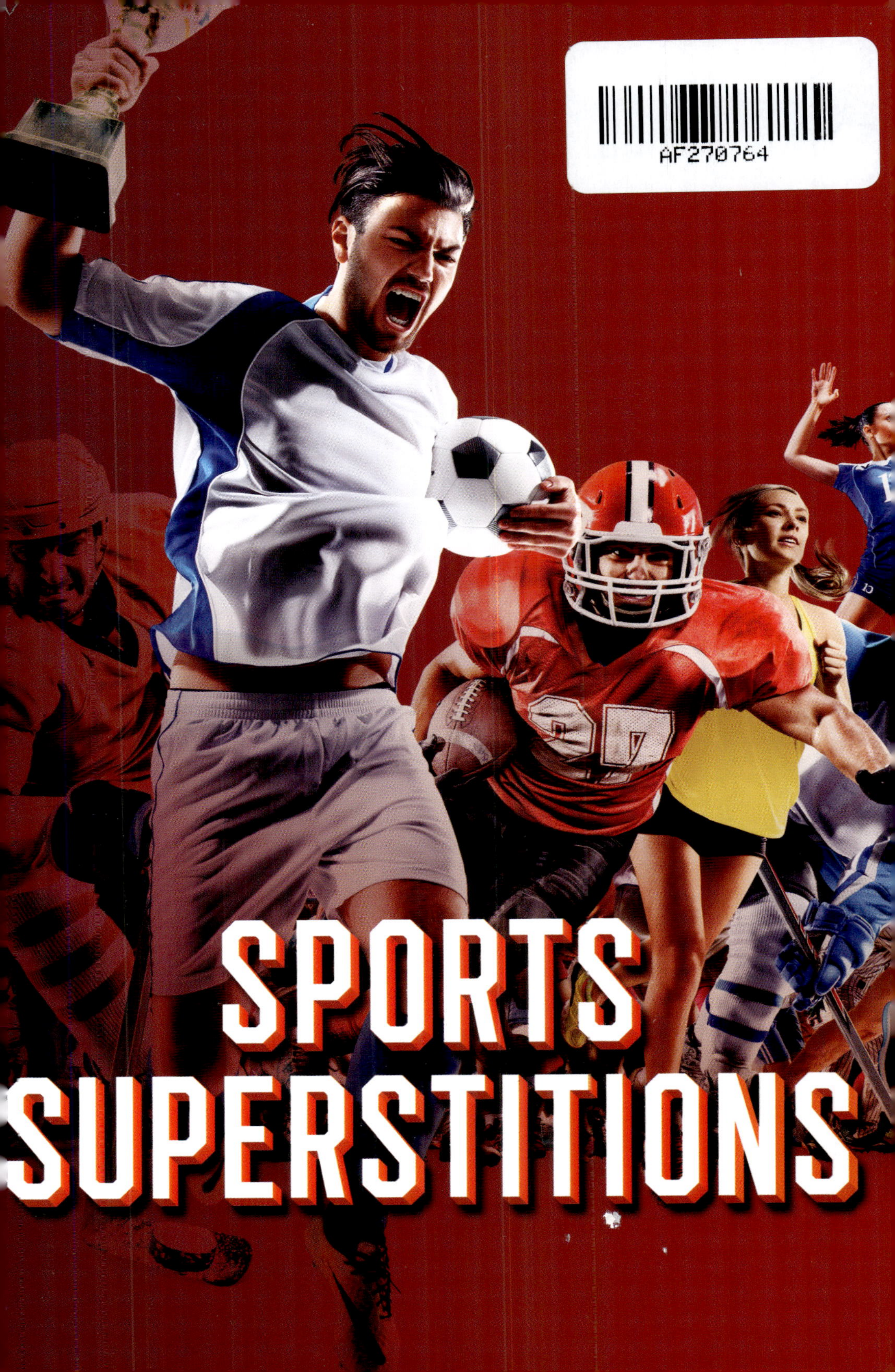
AF270764
SPORTS
SUPERSTITIONS

Copyright © 2020 by Saddleback Educational Publishing. All rights reserved. No part of this book may be reproduced in any form or by any means, electronic or mechanical, including photocopying, recording, scanning, or by any information storage and retrieval system, without the written permission of the publisher. SADDLEBACK EDUCATIONAL PUBLISHING and any associated logos are trademarks and/or registered trademarks of Saddleback Educational Publishing.

Photo credits: pages 8/9: Tim DeFrisco/Getty Images Sport via Getty Images; page 10: Tim DeFrisco/Getty Images Sport via Getty Images; pages 12/13: Quinn Rooney/Getty Images Sport via Getty Images; page 14: James Marvin Phelps/Shutterstock.com; page 15: Quinn Rooney/Getty Images Sport via Getty Images; page 17: Otto Greule Jr/Getty Images Sport via Getty Images; page 18: Steve Dykes/Getty Images Sport via Getty Images; page 18: Billion Photos/Shutterstock.com; page 19: Ronald Martinez/Getty Images Sport via Getty Images; page 20: STEFANY LUNA DE LINZY/Shutterstock.com; page 21: Mark Brown/Getty Images Sport via Getty Images; pages 22/23: Dennis Grombkowski/Getty Images Sport via Getty Images; page 24: Refugio Ruiz/Getty Images Sport via Getty Images; page 25: Chris Brunskill/Getty Images Sport via Getty Images; page 26: lazyllama/Shutterstock.com; page 26: Lars Baron/Getty Images Sport via Getty Images; page 27: Tom Pennington/Getty Images Sport via Getty Images; pages 28/29: Harry How/Getty Images Sport via Getty Images; page 30: Brian Bahr/Getty Images Sport via Getty Images; page 31: Ezra Shaw/Hulton Archive via Getty Images; page 31: Steve Cukrov/Shutterstock.com; page 31: Jeffrey B. Banke/Shutterstock.com; page 32: Kevin Hoffman/Getty Images Sport via Getty Images; page 33: Bruce Bennett/Getty Images Sport via Getty Images; page 35: Christopher Pasatieri/Getty Images Sport via Getty Images; page 36: Lisa Blumenfeld/Getty Images Sport via Getty Images; page 37: General Photographic Agency/Hulton Archive via Getty Images; page 39: Stuart Franklin/Getty Images Sport via Getty Images; page 40: Steve Powell/Getty Images Sport via Getty Images; page 41: Gary Newkirk/Getty Images Sport via Getty Images; page 42: Patrick Smith/Getty Images Sport via Getty Images; page 44: action sports/Shutterstock.com; page 46: Geoff Burke/Getty Images Sport via Getty Images; page 47: Rey Del Rio/Getty Images Sport via Getty Images; page 48: Jamie Squire/Getty Images Sport via Getty Images; page 53: Chris Graythen/Getty Images Sport via Getty Images; page 55: Kevin C. Cox/Getty Images Sport via Getty Images; page 55: Jim Rogash/Getty Images Sport via Getty Images

ISBN: 978-1-68021-744-5
eBook: 978-1-64598-050-6

Printed in Malaysia

24 23 22 21 20   1 2 3 4 5

TABLE OF CONTENTS

CHAPTER 1
FOR THE WIN

A tennis star wears dirty socks on the court. A quarterback carries a lucky rock. Athletes have many **superstitions**. These are beliefs. They are not based on fact. Often, superstitions do not make sense. But people still believe in them.

Balls bounce the wrong way. Players can trip. Bad weather happens. Athletes focus on what they can control. Some have personal superstitions. They often carry **charms**. A charm is a special item. It is thought to bring good luck.

Many athletes have **rituals**. These are actions done in special situations. The actions are always done the same way. They follow a certain order. Certain rituals are thought to bring luck. One player may always swing the bat five times. Another might eat certain foods before a game. Rituals often start as **habits**. A habit is an action a person does regularly. Habits are not usually done on purpose.

Sports fans have charms and rituals too. They may not wash a favorite jersey or hat. Some always sit in the same place. Can this help their team win? Many believe it does.

HOW SUPERSTITIONS START

Superstitions often start as part of a routine. Sometimes charms are a gift. Then players see a connection. Did the action or charm increase success? Soon a ritual is done every game. Other items or habits can be added. This can create a chain of rituals. Teammates notice. They think it is working. Before long, an entire team has a superstition.

CHAPTER 2
BASKETBALL

Basketball is a fast-paced sport. It requires great **skill**. But there is also luck involved. Some players believe in this more than others.

Michael Jordan was a talented basketball player. He was a shooting guard in college. Later he was **drafted** by the Chicago Bulls. Jordan kept wearing his shorts from college. These were his good luck charm. There was one problem though. They stuck out of the bottom of his Bulls uniform. Longer shorts were needed to cover them. This style became popular. Other players soon began wearing long shorts.

MICHAEL JORDAN

Mike Bibby played 1,001 games in the NBA. The point guard bit his fingernails. When **anxiety** struck, he chewed. Then a teammate saw. He gave Bibby some nail clippers. Using them helped the nervous player. Bibby trimmed his nails during time-outs. Soon it became a ritual.

Jerry Tarkanian was a college basketball coach. His teams were champions. During games, he chewed on a towel. This odd habit started in the 1950s. Tarkanian had dry mouth. A doctor told him that chewing on a wet towel might help. It did. Soon the coach noticed a connection. Chewing the towel led to big wins. A new superstition was formed.

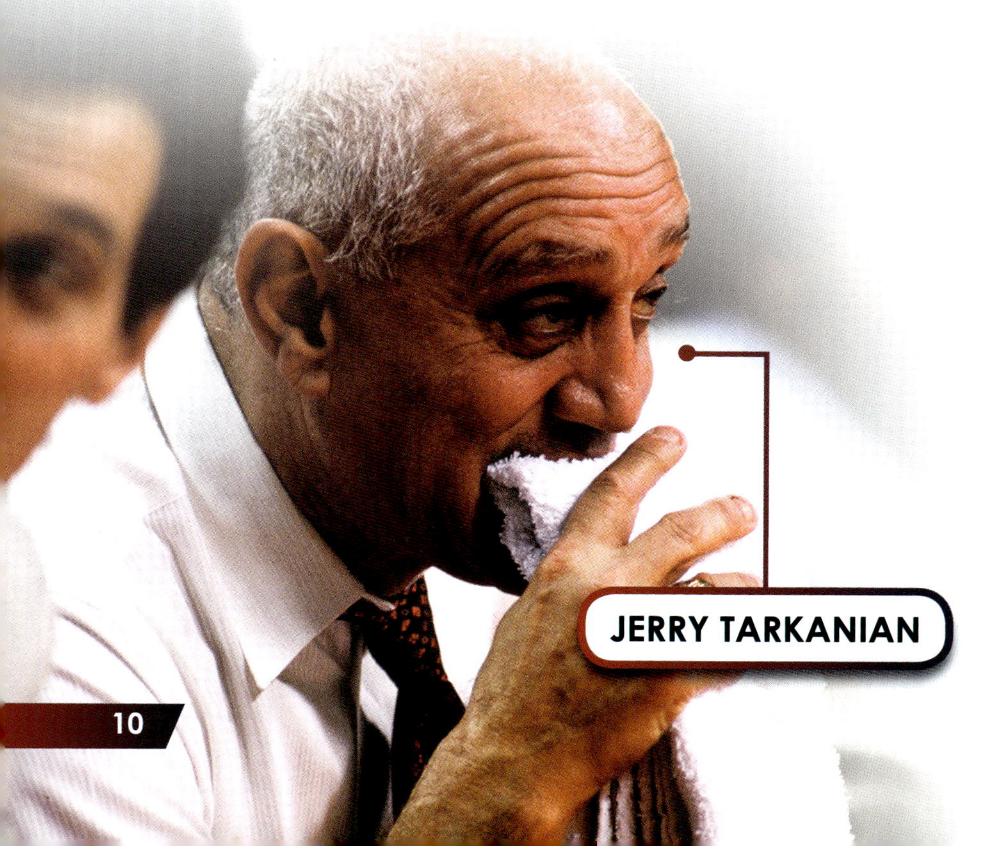

LeBron James joined the NBA in 2003. Fans call him "King James." In each game, he scores about 27 points. The athlete always chalks his hands before playing. He claps his hands together and blows on them. Chalk dust floats through the air. James also has a special handshake for each of his teammates. They shake before every game. This ritual is calming. It lets the king rule the court.

THE SCIENCE OF SUPERSTITIONS

Superstitions are common in sports. Most players have one. Some players have many. Two scientists were curious about this. They did a study in 2006. The scientists talked to almost 200 players. Most of them played soccer. Others played hockey and volleyball. All were professionals. About 80 percent said they were superstitious. Many had two or more rituals.

In 2010, other scientists did experiments. Four experiments were with golfers. Only 20 percent were not superstitious. Most golfers believed in good luck. Scientists gave them "lucky" golf balls. This superstition helped. The athletes played better. When golfers felt lucky, they were more confident. Their stress was reduced. With clear minds, their bodies worked better.

CHAPTER 3
TENNIS

Tennis is a high-speed sport. Players think quickly and move fast. One small action can make or break a **match**. There is a lot of **uncertainty**. Rituals may bring players luck.

Serena Williams is an American tennis player. She wins 85 percent of her matches. The star athlete has rituals. One involves the tennis ball. Before the first serve, she bounces it five times. Then she bounces it twice before the second serve. Williams is also known for her socks. They are not changed during a **tournament**. A tournament might last for two weeks.

SERENA WILLIAMS

Rafael Nadal comes from Spain. He plays men's singles tennis. At the beginning of 2019, he was **ranked** second best in the world. Nadal won gold at the 2008 Olympics. Before a match, he takes a cold shower. He then goes onto the court. There, water bottles are lined up. He drinks them in order. The pro also tucks his hair behind his ears before each serve.

A SUPERSTITIOUS BUNCH

In 2014, the news show *60 Minutes* did a poll on superstitions. About 54 percent of people said they were not superstitious. More than 40 percent said they were a little superstitious. Only 4 percent were very superstitious.

A different poll was done with sports fans. It found that 68 percent were superstitious. Fans were asked if they had rituals. About 10 percent said no and 20 percent said maybe. Almost 70 percent said yes. This means sports fans are up to 18 times more superstitious than other people.

Ana Ivanovic was a tennis player from Serbia. The star never stepped on tennis court lines. Before every match, she ate at the same restaurants. She used the same shower stalls too. Ivanovic also wore the same outfits. Her rituals may have helped at the 2008 French Open. That year, she came in first place.

CHAPTER 4
FOOTBALL

Football players are tough. They are also often superstitious. Brian Urlacher was a linebacker for the Chicago Bears. He had more than 1,000 tackles. Urlacher believed cookies helped him. Chocolate chip were his favorite. The athlete always ate two cookies. Then he took the field.

BRIAN URLACHER

Marshawn Lynch is a running back. He has a sweet tooth too. When Lynch played for the Seattle Seahawks, he ate Skittles before games. This ritual became famous. Lynch had many fans. They tossed Skittles onto the field when he scored. But the player's love of Skittles actually started years earlier. His mother gave him the candy before games. She said it would help him run fast.

College coach Les Miles also has a snack superstition. He coached Louisiana State University for many years. Before that, he played baseball. Sometimes it was boring. The right fielder would pick a few blades of grass and chew them. As a football coach, he started chewing grass again. His team started to win more. Miles's strange habit soon became a ritual.

Tom Brady might be the best quarterback in history. He plays for the New England Patriots. Brady holds dozens of records. This player always wears a lucky necklace. His wife gave it to him. At each game, Brady's wife makes a small altar. She includes photos of their children. It is for good luck.

Madden NFL is a popular video game. The player on the cover is thought to be cursed. Is this superstition true?

2000
BARRY SANDERS
Detroit Lions running back
Retired suddenly
CURSED

2001
EDDIE GEORGE
Tennessee Titans running back
Underperformed
CURSED

2004
MICHAEL VICK
Atlanta Falcons quarterback
Was injured and missed all but five games
CURSED

2005
RAY LEWIS
Baltimore Ravens linebacker
Made almost 150 tackles
NOT CURSED

2007
SHAUN ALEXANDER
Seattle Seahawks running back
Left the NFL
CURSED

2009
BRETT FAVRE
New York Jets quarterback
Had an injury and moved teams
CURSED

2011
DREW BREES
New Orleans Saints quarterback
Lost in the playoffs
CURSED

2015
RICHARD SHERMAN
Seattle Seahawks cornerback
Kept playing well
NOT CURSED

2017
ROB GRONKOWSKI
New England Patriots tight end
Had many injuries and only played eight games
CURSED

2018
TOM BRADY
New England Patriots quarterback
Won the Super Bowl
NOT CURSED

THE LUCKIEST PLAYS IN FOOTBALL

There have been many surprising football plays. People think good luck may have helped. One example was in 2008. The New York Giants went to the Super Bowl. David Tyree was a wide receiver. Quarterback Eli Manning threw him a pass. Tyree caught the ball. He caught it against his head. The Giants won. This play is called the "helmet catch."

In 2018, the Miami Dolphins were losing. They were behind by five points. There were seven seconds left. Ryan Tannehill was quarterback. He threw the ball. Kenny Stills made the catch. Stills passed the ball to DeVante Parker. Parker then threw it. Kenyan Drake ran the ball and scored a touchdown. The Dolphins won the game by one point. This play was named the "Miracle in Miami."

CHAPTER 5
SOCCER

Soccer is filled with superstitions. Teams headed to away games often travel by bus. If they win, players sit in the same bus seats. This is thought to be good luck. The seats stay the same until they lose. Some players believe their clothes bring them luck. Socks, cleats, and even underwear can be lucky. These items are worn game after game. Losing means it's finally time to do laundry.

Abby Wambach played with the U.S. women's soccer team. This star had several rituals. Before every game, she used the same bathroom stall. The forward also put her socks on in order. Cleats went on in order too. In 2015, Wambach's teammates voted her "Most Superstitious." That year, her team won the World Cup. She also led the U.S. Olympic team to two gold medals. These were in 2004 and 2012.

ABBY WAMBACH

Diego Maradona was a soccer player from Argentina. In 1997, he retired. Then he became a coach for Dorados de Sinaloa of Mexico. Maradona is superstitious. **Press conferences** must be held at the same place. This breaks soccer rules. The coach also walks around the field before a match. He takes photos of the space. Before every game, Maradona calls his daughters for good luck.

Soccer players run onto the field. They do this at the start of games. It happens again after halftime. For most this is fine. But Kolo Touré had a superstition. He needed to be the last onto the field. In 2009, he played for Arsenal. One of his teammates was injured. The player could not return to the field. Touré would not go back before him. Then the second half started. Arsenal had to start playing without Touré.

AT THE OLYMPICS

The Olympic Games happen every four years. Athletes need luck on their side. Jessie Diggins is a skier. She is on the U.S. women's team. Diggins puts glitter on her teammates. Each team member always wears braids. They also wear special socks. The team won gold at the 2018 Winter Olympics.

Karen Chen is a figure skater. She was at the 2018 games too. The skater placed 11th. Chen wears a lucky jade necklace. Before her routine, the athlete always gives her mom a big hug.

Olympic swimmer Michael Phelps had many rituals. Before a swim meet, he listened to music. It had to be certain songs. Before going into the pool, the Olympian swung his arms. He made circles with them three times. Phelps won 28 Olympic medals total. Of these, 23 were golds.

Yoshiaki Oiwa of Japan rides horses. He competed in the 2008 and 2012 Summer Olympics. Oiwa sprinkles salt for good luck. The salt goes on himself. It also goes on his horse.

CHAPTER 6
ICE HOCKEY

Many ice hockey players follow superstitions. Team members go onto the ice in a special order. The order must be the same each time. It is bad luck to step on team **logos**. Touching trophies is also bad luck.

Alex Rigsby is a hockey goalie. Her success might be due to a lucky tennis ball. Before games, she gets dressed. But it must be in a certain way. Then she tapes her stick. The team has warm-ups. After, Rigsby bounces her lucky ball. In college, the goaltender became team captain. It was the first time a goalie was captain of that team. In 2012, Rigsby joined the U.S. women's national team.

ALEX RIGSBY

Patrick Roy was another superstitious player. The goaltender played for the National Hockey League (NHL). He talked to the goalposts. Roy would also jump over lines on the ice. People say he was one of the best goalies in history.

Wayne Gretzky is called "the Great One." He played center in the NHL. The hockey **legend** scored 894 goals. That is more than any other player. Gretzky had a ritual. First, he drank a soda. It was washed down with ice water. Then came a sports drink. If extra luck was needed, Gretzky drank another soda.

Sidney Crosby plays center for the Pittsburgh Penguins. He has been an All-Star many times. Crosby is very superstitious. His hockey stick has to be a certain length. It has to be taped just right too. Only Crosby can then touch it. Otherwise, it has to be re-taped. The athlete also will not speak to his mom before games. Once when they did talk, he was injured.

PLAYOFF BEARDS

A hockey team started a superstition in the 1980s. The New York Islanders stopped shaving. They grew beards during the playoffs. It became a tradition. This tradition spread. Players in other sports do it too. It's called the "playoff beard."

There are simple rules. The playoffs or finals begin. Players can no longer shave. Their beards might be itchy. Hair gets caught in helmets. Trimming is allowed, but only after a loss. This can bring back good luck. A team can shave when it is eliminated. Finally, a team wins the championship. Those players often keep their beards. They wear them to celebrate.

WASHINGTON CAPITALS

CHAPTER 7
BASEBALL

In one baseball game, both teams throw about 150 pitches. Players each bat three to five times. There are many chances for good or bad luck.

Ervin Santana is a pitcher. He joined Major League Baseball in 2005. Santana has pitched in hundreds of games. Before every pitch, he does the same set of moves. The ball is held up to his nose. Then comes a deep breath. Now the pro is ready to play. This ritual calms his mind. It helps him throw **strikes**.

ERVIN SANTANA
Minnesota
HOME RU
BASEBALL AREN
BAS

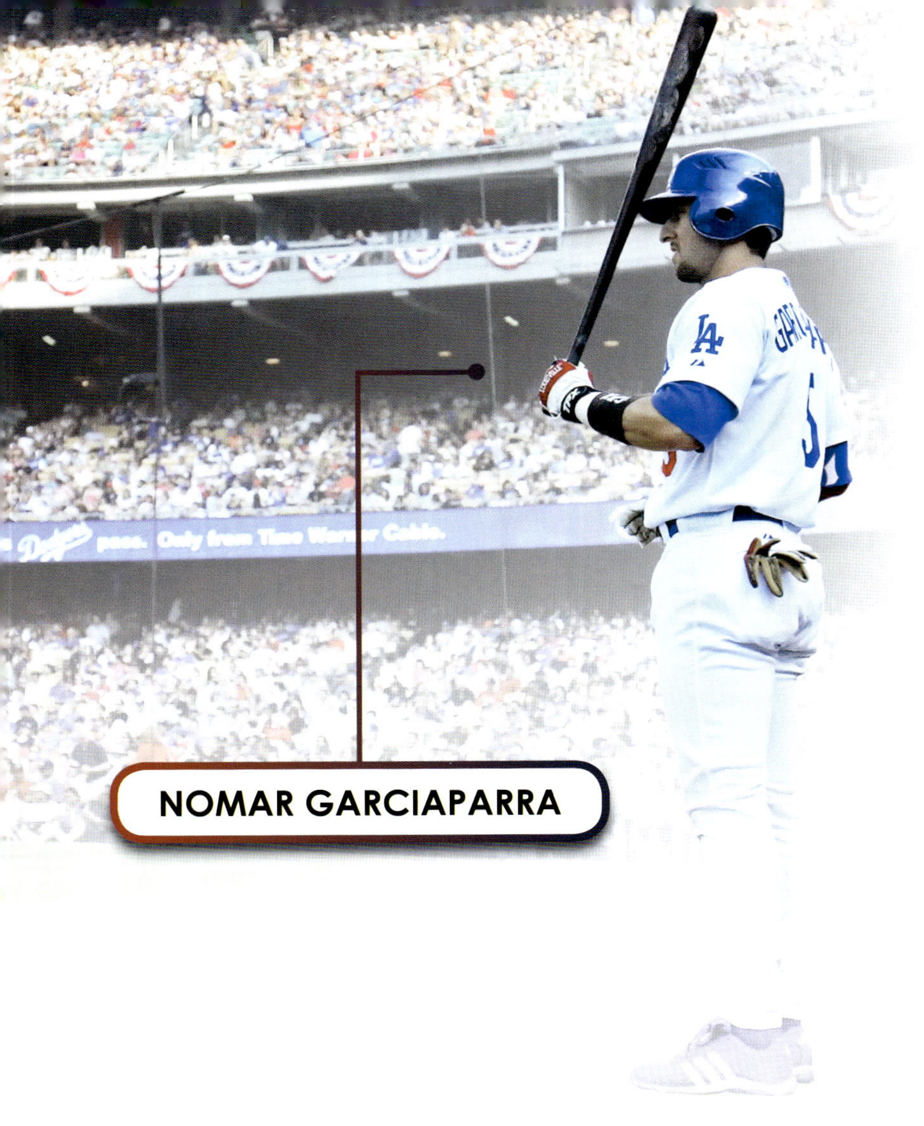

Infielder Nomar Garciaparra played in six All-Star games. Was this perhaps because of his ritual? It started when he stepped up to bat. First, he adjusted his arm band. Then he pulled at his gloves. The slugger tapped the base with his bat. Next, he touched the bat to his helmet. Finally, the infielder dug his cleats into the ground. Garciaparra hit 229 home runs in his career. He also won many awards.

Babe Ruth is a baseball legend. His 714 home runs are world famous. The big hitter had several superstitions. Ruth played in the outfield. Between innings, outfielders ran back to the **dugout**. On the way, he always stepped on second base. Teammates were also not allowed to use his bats. He believed each one held a certain number of hits. These were just for him.

AGAINST THE RULES

Some superstitions break the rules. Players get in trouble. Many times, it is because of good luck charms. This has happened in baseball. Julián Tavárez was a pitcher. In 2004, he was kicked out of a game. His lucky cap was too dirty. Nomar Garciaparra also got in trouble. The infielder kept dirtying his helmet. He even had to pay a fine. It was $4,500. Rules say uniforms must be clean. Caps and helmets cannot be dirty. However, many players like dirty gear. They believe these charms help them do well.

CHAPTER 8
GOLF

Golf moves at a slow pace. All is quiet on the green. This calm sport has its own superstitions.

Tiger Woods is one of the greatest golfers. He has over 80 wins on the Professional Golfers Association (PGA) Tour. Good luck charms are important to him. One is a red shirt. It is always worn during the final round of a tournament. This wasn't Woods's idea. His mother told him to do it. She says red is his power color.

TIGER WOODS

Jack Nicklaus is in the World Golf Hall of Fame. He was an important golfer. In his pocket, the competitor carried three coins. They could be quarters. Pennies were okay too. No matter what, there always had to be three. These were for good luck.

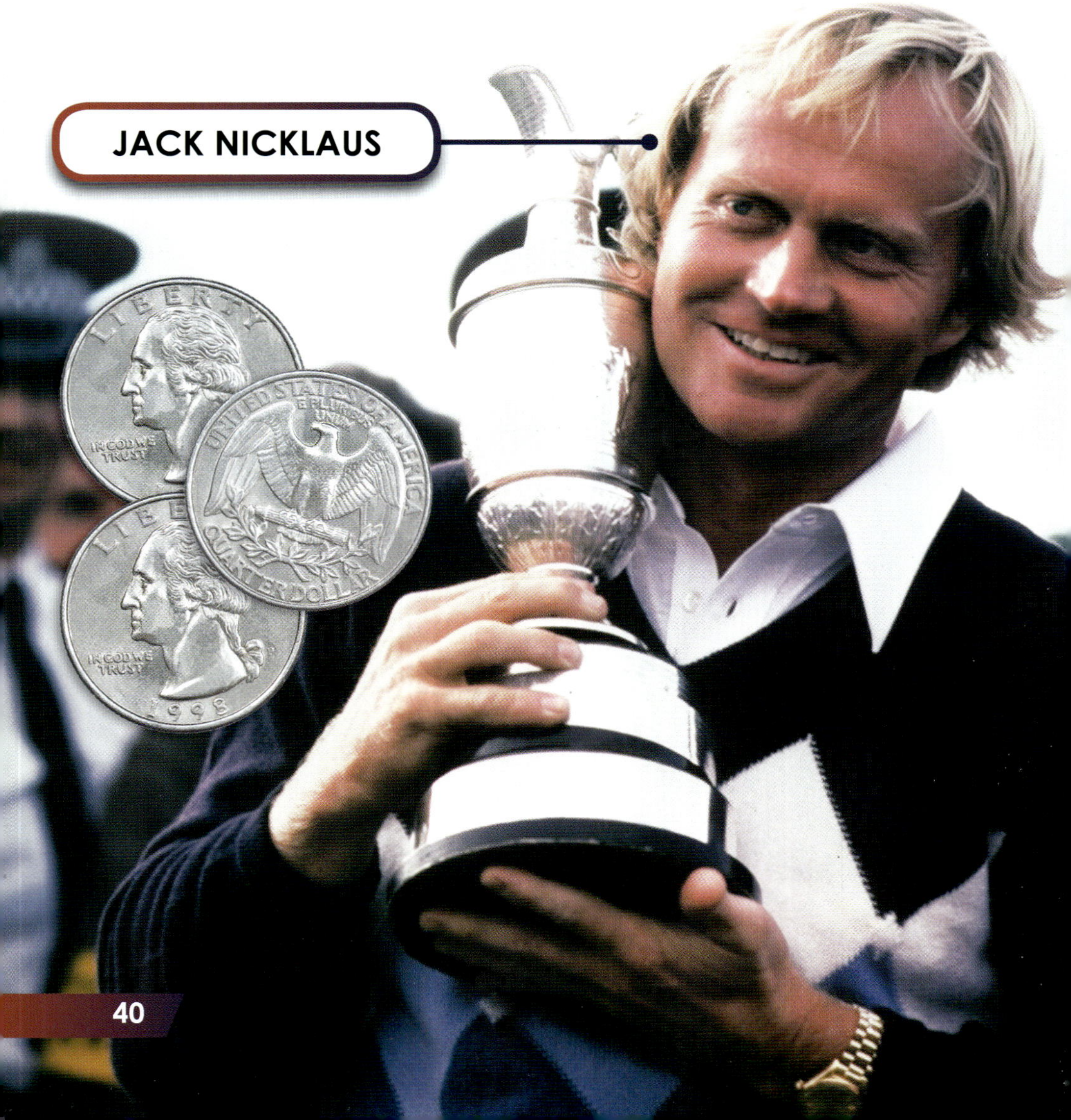

Chi-Chi Rodríguez is a golfer from Puerto Rico. The athlete has eight PGA Tour wins. He works with coins too. They are used to mark his putts. Rodríguez marks **birdies** with quarters. Other putts are marked with nickels. Sometimes the golfer needs extra good luck. A gold coin does the trick.

Ernie Els is a golfer from South Africa. He has won 19 times on the PGA Tour. This pro golfer has a **wasteful** superstition. After a birdie, he throws away the ball. He believes it has no more good luck left. Els played in the PGA Tour in 2013. The competitor threw away 260 balls.

Ben Crenshaw won 19 PGA Tour events. He also had a golf ball superstition. Crenshaw only played with certain balls. They could only have the numbers 1, 2, 3, or 4 on them. These were his lucky numbers.

LUCKY NUMBERS

Many people have lucky numbers. A British author wrote a book on this. He surveyed 30,000 people around the world. People said 7 was the luckiest number. It was followed by 3, 8, and 4. Ancient people also liked the number 7. This includes the ancient Greeks. They thought the spiritual world had three parts. The physical world had four parts. Together, that made seven.

People have unlucky numbers too. In China, the number 4 is very unlucky. In Chinese, the word meaning "four" sounds like another word. That word means "death." In Japan, the number 9 is unlucky. The Japanese word for "nine" sounds like the word for "suffering."

CHAPTER 9
NASCAR

NASCAR is a dangerous sport. Cars go 200 miles per hour. Sometimes they crash. A crash can end a race. It can also end a life. Many drivers are very superstitious. They may count on luck to protect them.

Peanuts are a favorite snack. But they are not allowed at NASCAR events. This superstition is from the 1930s. Back then, races were often held at fairgrounds. People ate peanuts. They dropped the shells. These got in the way of the racers. When there was a crash, there were peanut shells around. The shells became a symbol of bad luck.

REGISTER
INLAND☆CAL
.COM
KURT BUSCH
BOWYER
PEAK
ANTIFREEZE ☆ MOTOR OIL
15
CAMRY
WÜRTH
FUSION
VICKERS
55
55

Another racing superstition is very old. In 1920, a driver crashed and died. He had been driving a green car. The color green was then seen as unlucky. Some NASCAR drivers today use green cars. Many have had bad luck. Jeff Gordon crashed in a green car. It was one of his worst crashes.

In NASCAR, car number 13 is unlucky too. More than 70 drivers have had a car with the number. All have tried to reach the championship. A number-13 car has been in the series more than 400 times. But it has only won a series race once. That was in 1963.

Racing legend Dale Earnhardt had a bad-luck streak. For 19 years he had lost the Daytona 500. In 1998, he was given a good luck charm. There was a young girl named Wessa Miller. She was in a wheelchair. The Make-A-Wish Foundation helped her meet Earnhardt. Wessa gave him a lucky penny. Earnhardt glued it to his dashboard. Then he won the race.

UNLUCKY NUMBER 13

The number 13 is famous. It is the most common unlucky number. Buildings often do not have a 13th floor. Many airports lack a gate 13. Friday the 13th is seen as an unlucky day. Scientists are not sure why. Some think it is because of an ancient document. This is the Code of Hammurabi. The code is a list of laws. These laws cover all parts of life. There isn't a 13th law.

CHAPTER 10
FAN SUPERSTITIONS

Sports fans want their teams to win. Some think they can help. Many fans have charms. Others have rituals. Superstitions are followed at home and at games. They can go on for years.

One superstition is clothing. Fans may have lucky jerseys. Some might always wear the same hat. Often, these lucky clothes must match the team's colors.

Sitting in the same spot is also popular. This can be a lucky chair at home. At stadiums, fans buy tickets in the same seats. If their team is winning, they cannot get up. Others think moving can bring good luck. That's for when the team falls behind. Changing the channel can work too.

Superstitious fans might only watch games with certain people. They have lucky friends or family members. No one else is invited. During a game, they must eat the same food. The same drinks are served too.

Many fans watch what they say. It is bad luck to talk about losing. But it is even more unlucky to talk about winning. Sports **broadcasters** often follow these beliefs.

Some fans think they are very lucky. They have to watch the game for their team to win. These fans never miss a game. Another fan superstition is the opposite. The fans cannot watch the game. If they do, they might **jinx** it.

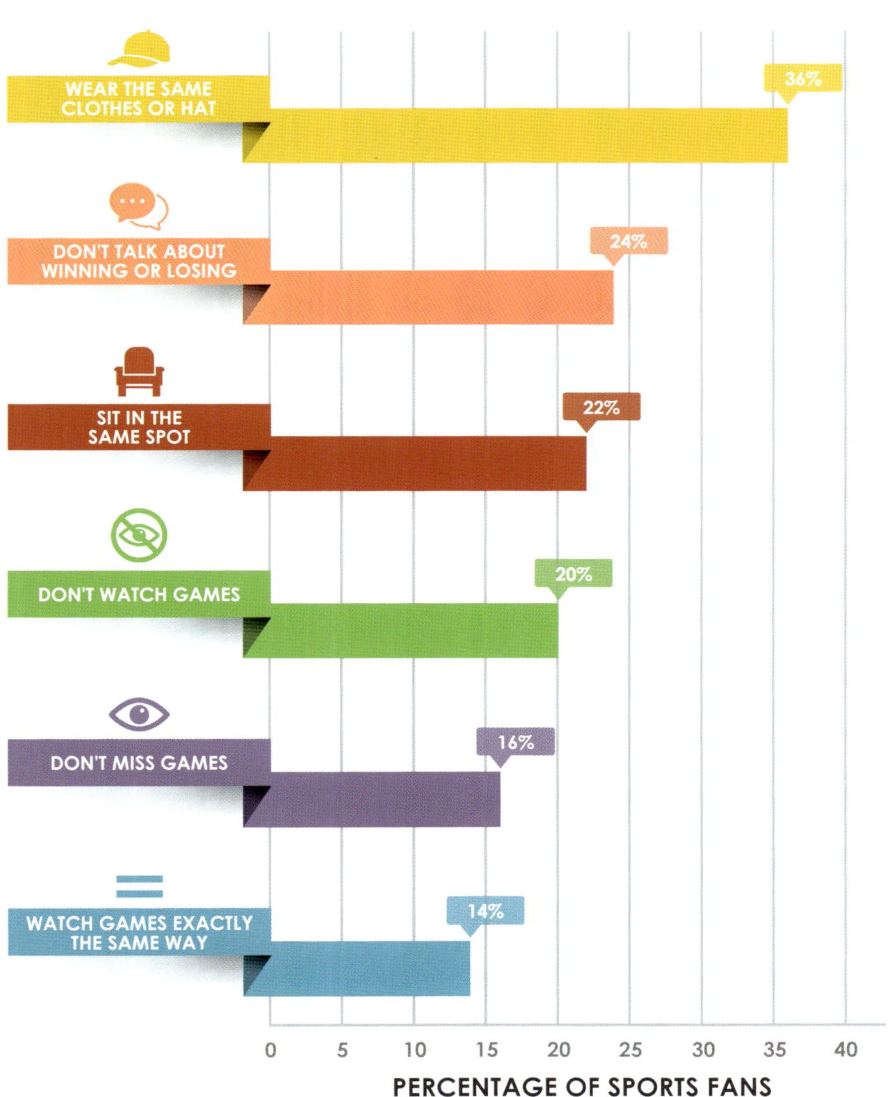

MOST COMMON FAN SUPERSTITIONS
More than 2,000 sports fans took a survey. The survey shows the most common superstitions.
WEAR THE SAME CLOTHES OR HAT
36%
DON'T TALK ABOUT WINNING OR LOSING
24%
SIT IN THE SAME SPOT
22%
DON'T WATCH GAMES
20%
DON'T MISS GAMES
16%
WATCH GAMES EXACTLY THE SAME WAY
14%
0
5
10
15
20
25
30
35
40
PERCENTAGE OF SPORTS FANS

BUFFALO BILLS FANS

THE MOST SUPERSTITIOUS FANS

A survey was done with thousands of sports fans. The survey said NFL fans are the most superstitious. Different NFL teams have varying levels of superstitious fans. Another study talked to 1,000 NFL fans. It put fans of the Buffalo Bills at the top of the list. The Bills started playing in 1960. They have won two conference championships. Buffalo has been to four Super Bowls. But they lost each time.

The NFL study ranked New England Patriots fans as some of the least superstitious. Their team has won six championships. They have been to a record 11 Super Bowls. The Patriots have won six of them. This includes the 2019 game.

NEW ENGLAND PATRIOTS

GLOSSARY

ANXIETY
worry or fear about what might happen

BIRDIE
a score that is one under the number of strokes a golfer is expected to take to finish a hole

BROADCASTER
a person who shares information on radio or TV

CHARM
an object thought to bring good luck

DRAFT
to select a player to be on a professional sports team

DUGOUT
a low shelter on the side of a baseball field where players and coaches sit

HABIT
an action that a person repeats regularly

JINX
to cause bad luck for someone or something

LEGEND
a person famous for doing something well

LOGO
a design that appears on a team's uniforms, arena, and other products

MATCH
a game or contest

PRESS CONFERENCE
a meeting during which someone gives information and reporters are allowed to ask questions

RANK
to be in a certain position among others who are being judged for similar athletic skills

RITUAL
a series of actions performed during special situations that are done the same way every time

SKILL
knowledge and experience needed to do something well

STRIKE
a missed pitch

SUPERSTITION
a belief that certain events or things will bring good or bad luck

TOURNAMENT
a series of games in which teams compete for a prize

UNCERTAINTY
doubt about what may happen

WASTEFUL
using more than necessary

INCREDIBLE COMEBACKS

HURRICANE STRENGTH

In each baseball game, almost 150 pitches are thrown. Pitchers tend to have injuries, often from overuse of certain muscles.

Pitches average 92 miles per hour. That is the speed of hurricane winds. Pitchers want to throw fast. Speed makes balls harder to hit. Over the years, pitchers have learned to throw faster. But this is harder on their bodies. Muscle strains and tears happen more often.

WORLD SERIES DROUGHTS

Baseball teams often go through droughts. In sports, a drought is a period of time a team goes without reaching a goal, like making it to a championship game. Many teams have had long World Series droughts. But some droughts end in comebacks. The following graph shows how long it took some MLB teams to overcome their droughts.

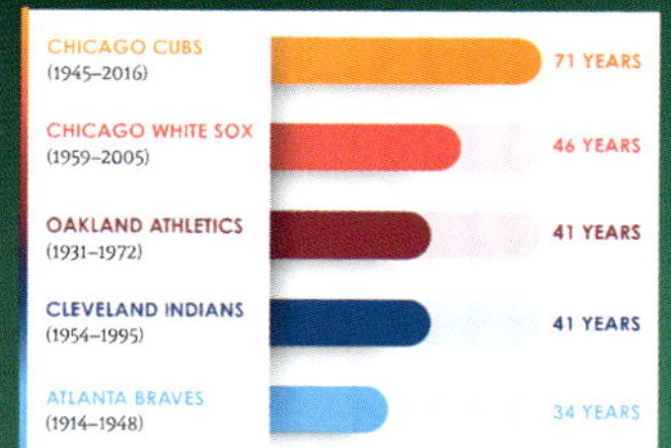

Sue Bird is in the WNBA. She plays point guard. From 2007 to 2013, the player had a rough time. During those years, Bird had multiple injuries. The athlete had surgeries on her knee and hip. A broken nose needed surgery too. Each operation meant months of healing time. In 2013, the sportswoman did not play. Every day, she worked on recovering.

Then Bird came back better than ever. She played in All-Star games. These were in 2014 and 2015. At the 2016 Olympic Games, the athlete won gold. Her game stayed strong. Bird was an All-Star in 2017 and 2018 too.

CHAPTER 5
FOOTBALL

Football is a full-contact sport. This means players tackle each other. Athletes have to be tough.

J.J. Watt is a Houston Texans star. He was in the Pro Bowl every year from 2012 to 2015. Then the athlete needed back surgery. The defensive end missed most games in 2016. Watt spent his time in recovery.

OR MORE TITLES AND INFORMATION ⟶

space∞™

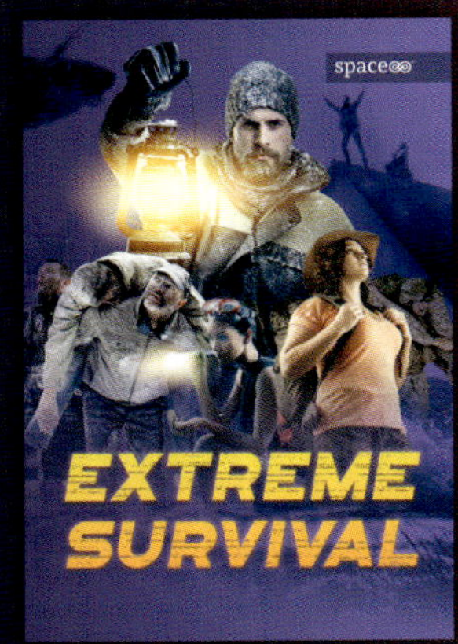

9781680217483

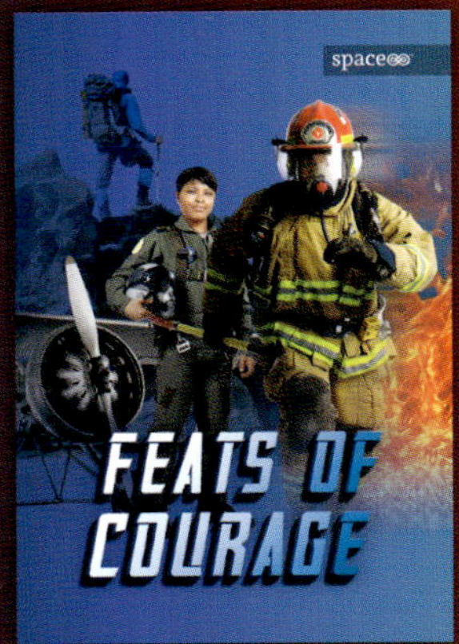

9781680217476

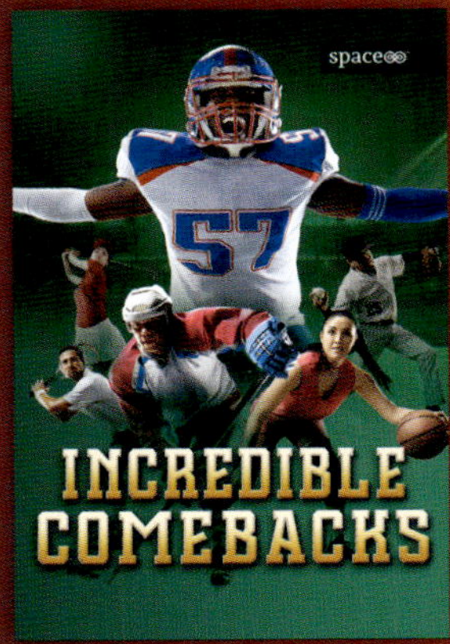

9781680217490

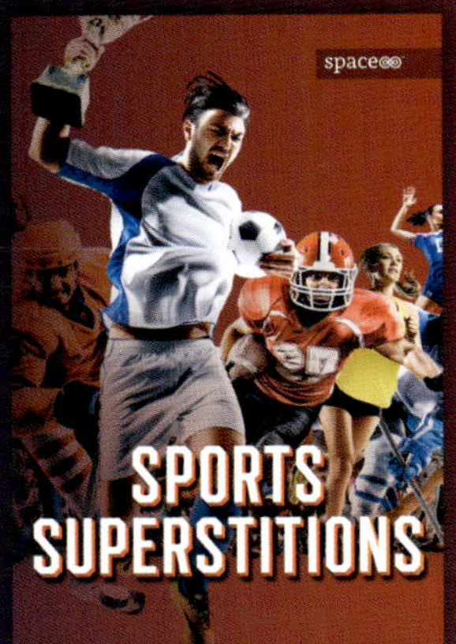

9781680217445

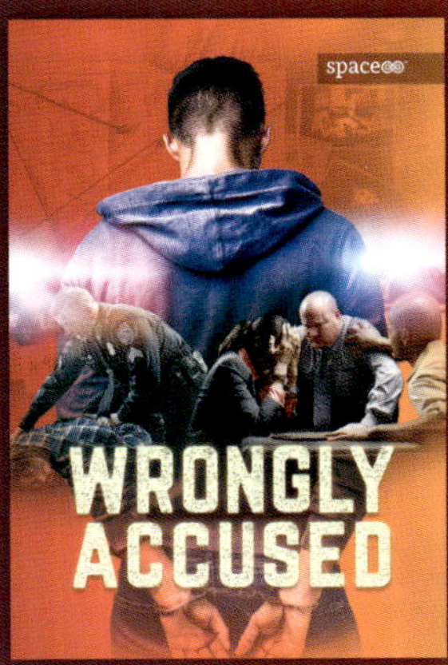

9781680217452

MORE TITLES COMING SOON

sdlback.com/Space-8